Kylie Jean

Party Craft Queen

by Marne Ventura and Marci Peschke
illustrated by Tuesday Mourning

PICTURE WINDOW BOOKS
a capstone imprint

Editor: Shelly Lyons
Designer: Tracy Davies McCabe
Craft Project Creator: Marcy Morin
Photo Stylist: Sarah Schuette
Art Director: Nathan Gassman
Production Specialist: Laura Manthe

Picture Window Books are published by Capstone,
1710 Roe Crest Drive, North Mankato, Minnesota 56003
www.capstonepub.com

Library of Congress Cataloging-in-Publication Data
Ventura, Marne and Marci Peschke.
Kylie Jean party craft queen / by Marne Ventura and
Marci Peschke.
pages cm — (Nonfiction picture books. Kylie Jean
craft queen)
Includes bibliographical references and index.
Audience: Age 6-9.
Audience: Grades K to 3.
Summary: "Introduces crafts related to the book Kylie
Jean Party Queen, by Marci Peschke"— Provided
by publisher.
ISBN 978-1-4795-2191-3 (library binding)
1. Handicraft—Juvenile literature. 2. Parties—Juvenile
literature. 3. Party decorations—Juvenile literature. I.
Peschke, M. (Marci). Party queen. II. Title.
TT160.V4485 2014
 745.5—dc2   2013034939

Photo Credits
All photos by Capstone Studio/Karon Dubke
Design elements: Shutterstock

Printed in the United States of America in Brainerd, Minnesota.
092013   007770BANGS14

Table of Contents

Y'all are invited to a party ... a crafting party! This book will show you how to create everything from invitations to favors. First make the party crowns. A queen can never have too many crowns! What does a girl wear with a crown to her best friend's party? A sparkly necklace, of course! You can put it together yourself by gathering the supplies and following the super easy directions in my party craft book. Let's get started!

TOOLS NEEDED

- cellophane tape
- hot glue gun
- markers
- paintbrush
- paper clips
- pencil
- ruler
- scissors
- sewing needle
- sharp knife
- single hole punch
- tempera paint
- toothpicks
- white glue

TIPS

- Before starting a project, read all of the steps and gather all of the supplies needed.
- Work on newspaper or paper towels.
- Ask an adult to help you use a hot glue gun and sharp tools.
- Give glue and paint plenty of time to dry before handling a project.

Kylie's Overnight Bag

I love this darlin' sleepover bag! You can use any bag to make it, but if your bag is pink, then you've picked my favorite color. Using glue to attach your hearts makes this project super quick and easy. That leaves you more time to pack for the party!

You will need:

- 2, 8-inch (20-centimeter) square sheets of white paper
- scissors
- 2, 8-inch (20-cm) felt squares
- pencil
- white glue
- reusable fabric shopping bag
- rhinestones
- 16-inch (41-cm) length of wide ribbon
- ruler

Optional:
- glitter foam stickers
- gemstone chain
- glitter glue

1. From paper, cut a heart shape. To make the heart shape the same on both sides, fold the paper down the middle, and cut both sides at once. Make a second smaller heart as well.

2. Open the folded paper hearts. Place the paper patterns on the felt and trace around them. Cut out.

3. Glue the hearts to the bag. Glue rhinestones onto the hearts.

4. Glue a length of ribbon to the bag about 1 inch (2.5 cm) above the hearts.

Optional: Apply glitter foam stickers, such as stars and a crown, around the hearts. Add a gemstone chain on top of the ribbon. Write your name with glitter glue.

1

2

3

4

Optional

7

Ribbon Hair Clip

What's more fun than a soda pop from the gas station? Using the bottle cap to make this super cute hair clip. When creating this clip, you get to use glitter!

You will need:

- plastic bottle cap
- white glue
- glitter
- 3 pieces of thin ribbon
- 2 pieces of wide ribbon
- 12 inches (31 cm) of thread
- hair barrette
- scissors
- hot glue

Optional:
- rhinestone

1. Glue glitter to the top of the bottle cap.

2. Glue a thin ribbon to the center of each of the wide ribbons.

3. When the glue is dry, fold each of the wide ribbons to make a loop and place one over the other to form a bow. Wrap the thread around the spot where the ribbons cross and around the top of the open barrette. Tie tightly with two knots. Cut off the end of the thread.

4. Use the third thin ribbon to cover the thread. Tie it twice at the base of the loops. Trim the ends to match the other ribbons.

5. Use a glue gun to attach the bottle cap to the center of the bow.

Optional: Hot glue a rhinestone to the top of the bottle cap.

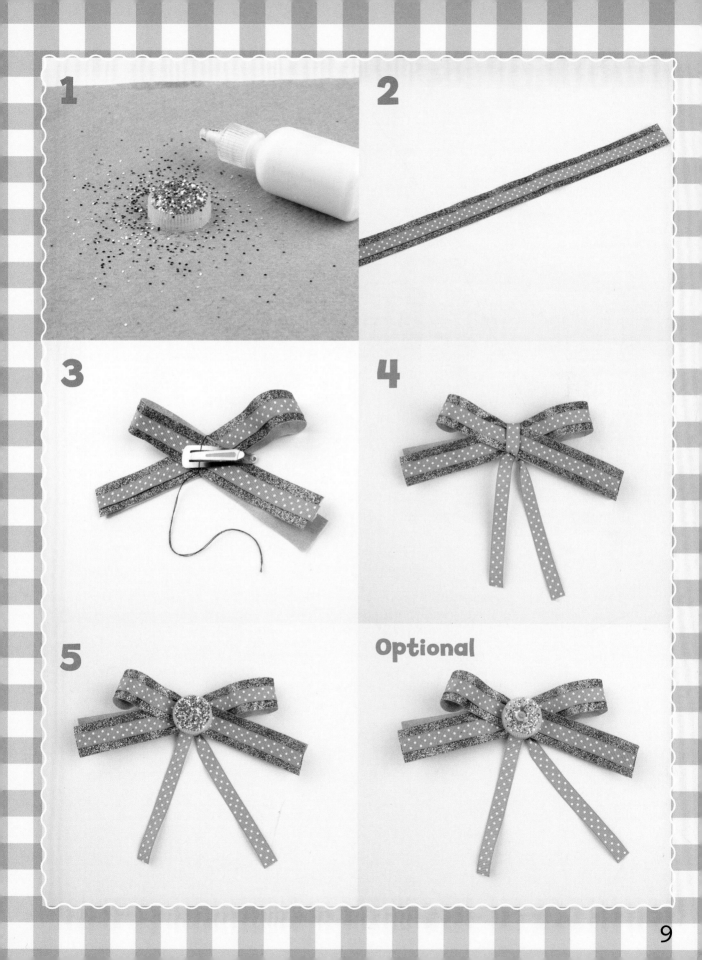

1

2

3

4

5

Optional

9

Toothbrush Tote

Beauty queens need beautiful smiles! Make this tote to store your toothbrush when you're away overnight. I know you'll love the easy way the tote rolls right up. Tie it with a bow, and off you go!

You will need:

- 12x12-inch (30x30-cm) washcloth
- hot glue
- ruler
- scissors
- 1 yard (.91 meter) of wide grosgrain ribbon

1. Fold the long end of the washcloth one-third of the way up. Use the glue gun to join the right edge of the fold together. To make four pockets, join the fold with glue in three lines, working from the right edge to the left. The glue lines will be 3 inches (7.6 cm) apart. Then glue the left edge.

2. Cut a V-shape at each end of the ribbon. Fold it in half. Glue the fold of the ribbon to the center of one side of the washcloth.

3. Put your toothbrush and toothpaste in the pockets.

4. Roll up and tie with the ribbon.

1

2

3

4

11

Party Gift Box

Sometimes a pretty package is just as nice as the present inside. When you make this sparkly box and give it to someone, she can reuse it!

You will need:

- box with a lid, about 4x4x2 inches (10x10x5 cm)
- tempera paint
- paintbrush
- 2 soup cans
- glitter
- ruler
- 48 inches (122 cm) of wide ribbon
- scissors
- white glue
- paper clips
- tissue paper

optional:
- rhinestones

1. Paint your gift box and lid. Set them on the cans to dry.

2. Repeat until the box and lid are the color you want. While the last coat of paint is still wet, sprinkle the box and lid with glitter. Let dry.

3. Measure and cut the ribbon to fit the lid. Leave an extra ½ inch (1.3 cm) on each end to fold over the edges of the lid. Glue the ribbon onto the lid. Clamp the ends in place with paper clips.

4. Place the lid on a can until the glue dries.

5. Repeat step 3 to make a cross on the box. Let dry.

6. Make a bow and glue it to the lid where the ribbons cross. Line the box with matching tissue paper.

Optional: Glue rhinestones onto the ribbon and bow.

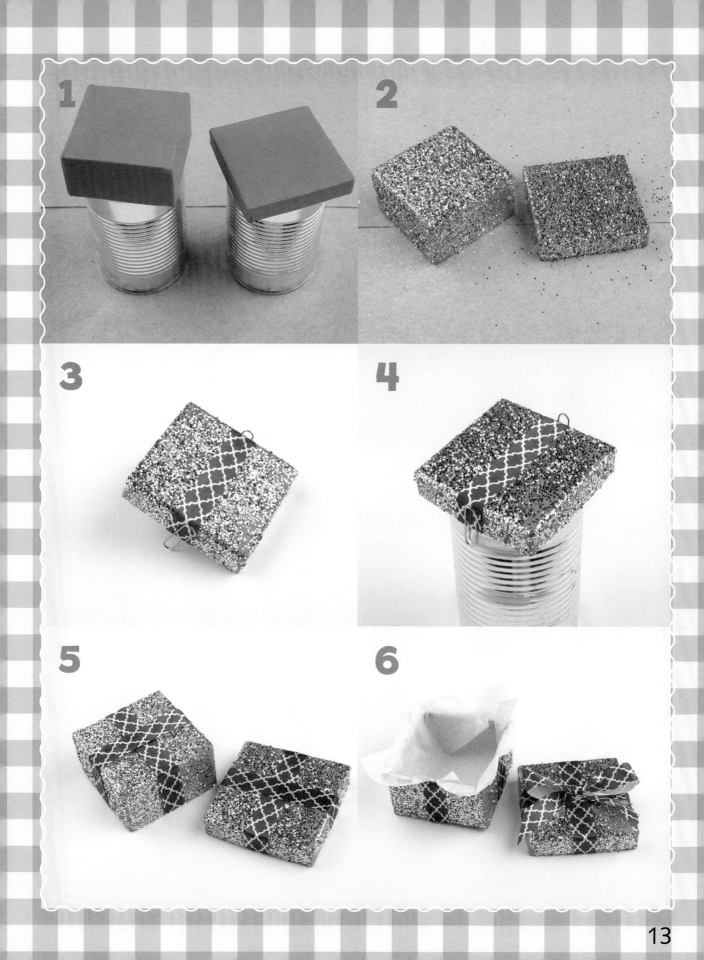

Rhinestone Bow Necklace

This craft project is so glamorous. Make it as a gift for a special friend. Your friend will feel like a movie star wearing something so sparkly!

You will need:

- small metal jump ring
- hot glue
- one bow tie pasta
- silver paint
- paintbrush
- 12 or more tube pasta pieces
- toothpick
- silver glitter
- 6 feet (1.8 meters) of thread
- sewing needle
- 28 beads
- white glue

1. Use a glue gun to attach the ring to the back of a bow tie pasta piece. The hole of the ring should face the points of the bow. Let dry.

2. Paint the tube pasta silver. To hold the tube pasta while you paint, stick a toothpick into the tube and hold the end. While the paint is still wet, roll the tube in silver glitter. Let dry.

3. Paint the bow tie silver. Sprinkle it with glitter while the paint is still wet. Let dry.

4. Thread a needle that is thin enough to go through the beads and long enough to go through the tubes. Tie the ends together with two knots. Loop the end around a toothpick. String four beads onto the thread.

5. String half of the tubes and beads onto the thread. Alternate two beads with one tube. String the bow tie. String the rest of the beads and tubes, using the same pattern. Remove the needle and tie two or three knots. Remove the toothpick. Trim the ends.

6. To keep the bow tie flat, glue it to the two middle beads with white glue. Let dry.

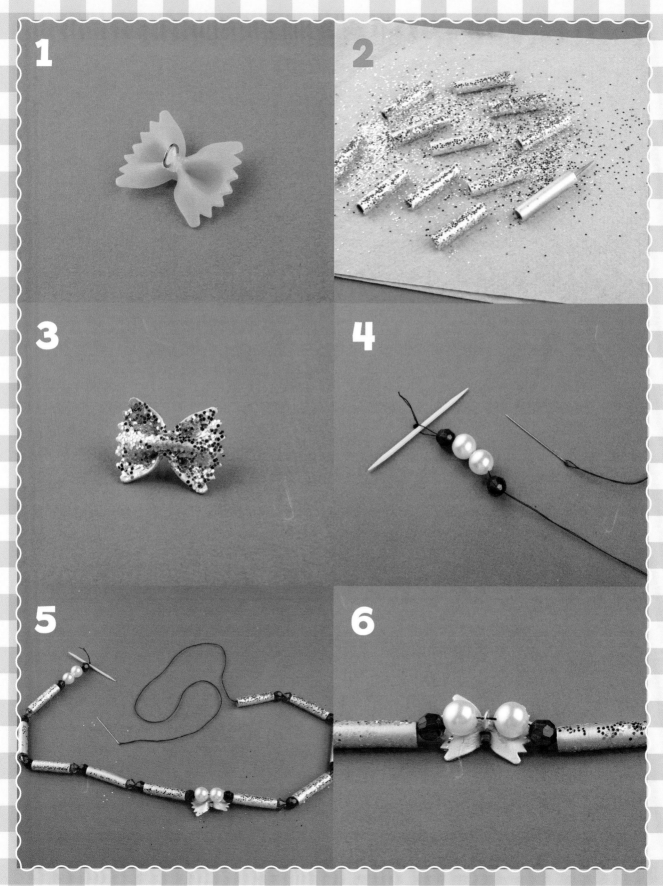

Princess Party Invitations

These are the most adorable invitations ever! You can make them all by yourself. I practiced writing down the party information ahead of time so I wouldn't make any mistakes. You can too!

You will need:

- 8½x11-inch (22x28-cm) silver card stock sheet
- scissors
- ruler
- 3, 8½x11-inch (22x28-cm) pink glitter paper sheets
- white glue
- 5x7-inch (13x18-cm) blank cards and matching envelopes
- 3, 8½x11-inch (22x28-cm) pink paper sheets
- rhinestones
- glitter glue
- markers
- glitter stickers

1. For each invitation, cut a crown shape from silver card stock. Start with a 3 ½-inch (8.9-cm) square.

2. For each invitation, cut a 4 ½-inch (11-cm) square of pink glitter paper. Glue it to the center of the front of the card.

3. For each invitation, cut a 4-inch (10-cm) square of pink paper. Cut the corners so they are round. Glue each rounded square to the center of each pink glitter square.

4. Glue each crown to the rounded square.

5. For each invitation, cut a pink glitter paper heart. Start with a 1 ¾-inch (4.4-cm) square of pink glitter paper.

6. Glue a heart to each crown. Glue rhinestones to the points of each crown.

7. With glitter glue, write "Princess Party" on the front of each card.

8. Write the party information on the inside of each card. Add glitter stickers to fill any empty space on the inside of the card.

1

2

3

4

5

6

7

PRINCESS

PARTY

8

Kylie Jean's
Princess Party!

Date: Saturday, June 26th

Time: 2:00 p.m.

Place: Kylie Jean's house

R.S.V.P.: to Kylie Jean's momma
by June 18th

Come to
Cara's Party!

Pin the Bow on the Gift

This is a craft project and a game! I bet you already have all of the supplies you'll need. Remember, no peeking while playing Pin the Bow on the Birthday Gift!

You will need:
- 7, 6-inch (15-cm) squares of scrapbook paper
- white glue
- 18x12-inch (46x30-cm) foam board
- scissors
- ruler
- 4 rolls of wide ribbon
- 1 sheet of card stock
- colored markers
- cellophane tape

1. Glue the scrapbook paper squares onto the foam board. There will be three across the top, and three across the bottom. Place one in the center.

2. Cut 2 lengths of ribbon, each 6 inches (15 cm). Glue two to the middle square, so the ribbons cross in the center.

3. For each party guest, tie a ribbon bow.

4. For each party guest, cut a 1-inch (2.5-cm) circle of card stock. With marker, write a guest's name on each circle. Place dots along the edge of each circle.

5. Tape each circle to a bow. Place a circle of tape on the back of each bow to play the game.

Hint:
To play Pin the Bow on the Gift, hang the board on a wall or fence. Blindfold a guest with a scarf, and give her a stick-on bow. Twirl her around, and point her toward the board. She will try to pin the bow on spot where the ribbons cross. The guest whose bow is closest wins.

Stamped Party Favor Bags

Favors are fun! Guests love to get them, and you'll think making these favor bags is a real treat. Personalizing them with each guest's name makes them extra special too.

You will need:

- potato
- sharp knife
- marker
- acrylic or tempera paint
- paintbrush
- pink lunch bags
- marker
- treats
- 16 inches (41 cm) of wide ribbon for each bag
- hole punch
- scissors

optional:
- about 9 sequins for each bag
- white glue

1. Pick two simple shapes to go with your party theme. Ask an adult to cut the potato in half. With marker, draw a shape on each cut side of the potato.

2. Ask and adult to cut away the potato around each of the shapes.

3. Brush paint on the stamps, and stamp the bags.

4. Write a guest's name on each bag with marker.

5. Fill each bag with treats.

6. Fold the top down about 1 inch (2.5 cm). Punch two holes in the center of the fold.

7. Cut the ends of the ribbon diagonally. Put the ribbon through the two holes. Tie a bow on the front to hold the bag closed.

Optional: Glue sequins to the front of each bag.

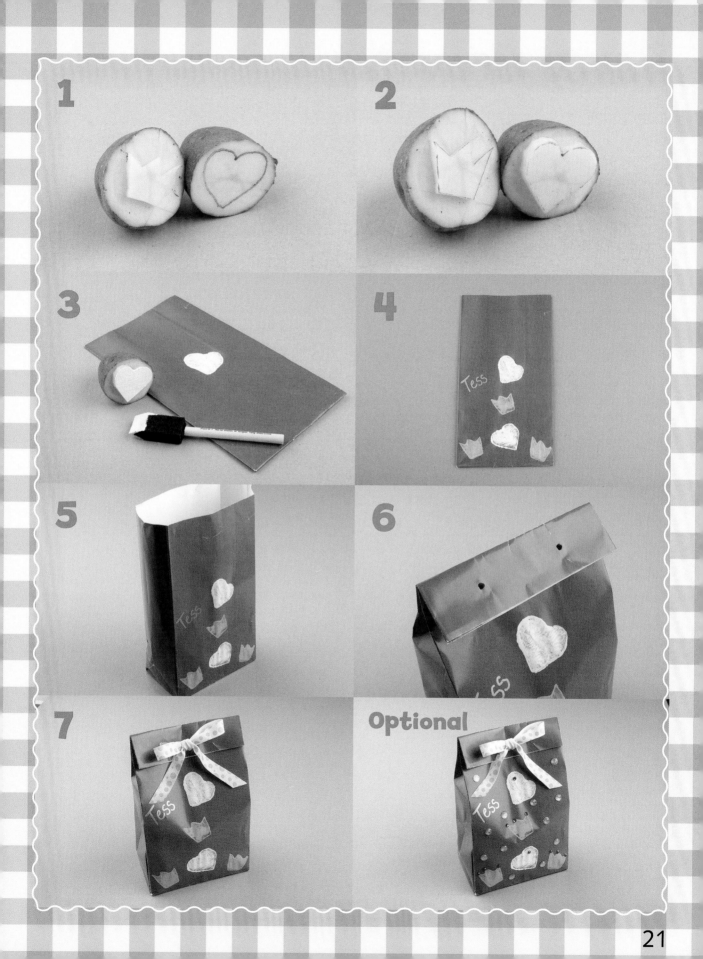

1

2

3

4

5

6

7

Optional

Party Crowns

Her majesty has spoken, and every guest is a queen! Each girl will feel like royalty in her own party crown. I put each guest's initial on her crown, so each girl knows which crown is hers.

You will need:

- 4½x7-inch (11x18-cm) white paper square
- ruler
- scissors
- 4½x7-inch (11x18-cm) pink felt
- pencil
- 4½x3½-inch (11x8.9-cm) purple felt
- white glue
- headband
- heavy book
- rhinestones
- letter stickers

1. Fold the paper in half so that it's 3½ inches (8.9 cm) by 4½ (11 cm). Cut a crown pattern from paper. The fold will be the bottom of the crown.

2. Fold the pink felt like you did the paper. Trace the crown shape onto the felt.

3. Cut out the felt crown.

4. Use the paper crown pattern to cut out a single crown from the purple felt. Now trim about ½ inch (1.3 cm) away from the purple crown, so it fits inside the pink crown. Glue it to the front side of the pink felt crown.

5. Fold the bottom of the crown around the headband. Cut a small notch on each end of the fold to let the headband curve downward. Glue the folded crown together. Place a heavy book on the crown. Let dry.

6. Glue the rhinestones to the front of the crown. Add a letter sticker to the middle of the crown to represent the guest's first name.

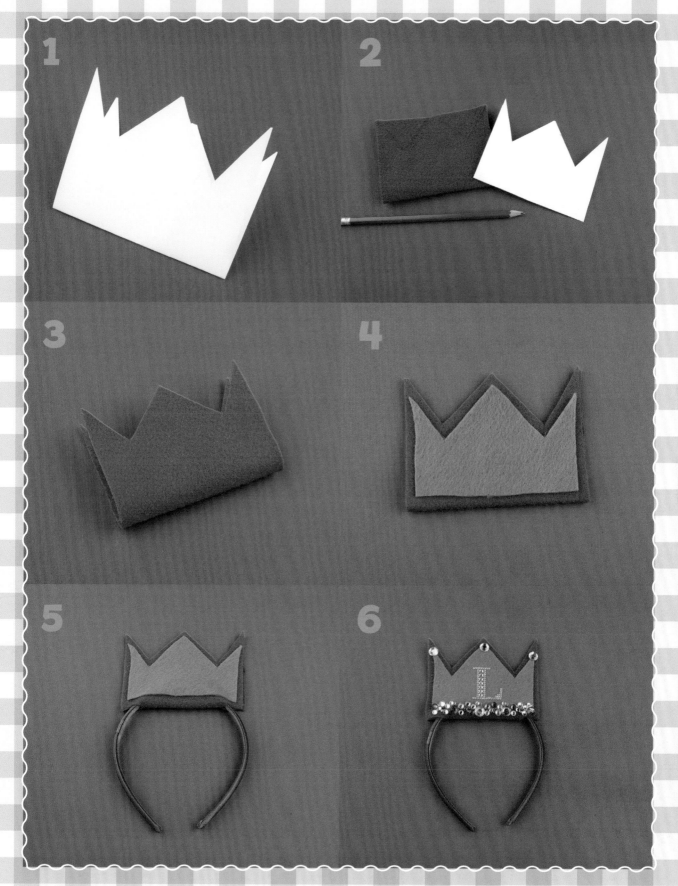

23

Baby Blanket Milk Shake

If you have a new baby in your family like I do, then this project is for you! Follow the directions to make your baby gift look like a yummy milk shake.

You will need:
- 29x29-inch (74x74-cm) fleece baby blanket
- 16-ounce (454-gram) plastic cup
- 1½-inch (3.8-cm) fuzzy pom-pom
- 14x4-inch (36x10-cm) glitter paper
- scissors
- ruler
- hot glue
- straw

1. Fold the blanket in half lengthwise. Fold it lengthwise again.

2. Roll up the blanket tightly.

3. Place it inside the cup. The top should stick up so it looks like swirled ice cream.

4. Push the pom-pom into the center of the rolled blanket top, so it looks like a cherry.

5. From the glitter paper, cut a 12-inch (30-cm) strip that's about 2¾ inches (7 cm) wide. The strip should have a slight arch.

6. Starting with one end of the glitter paper strip, glue the strip to the cup. Cut a straw in half and add it to the top of the milk shake.

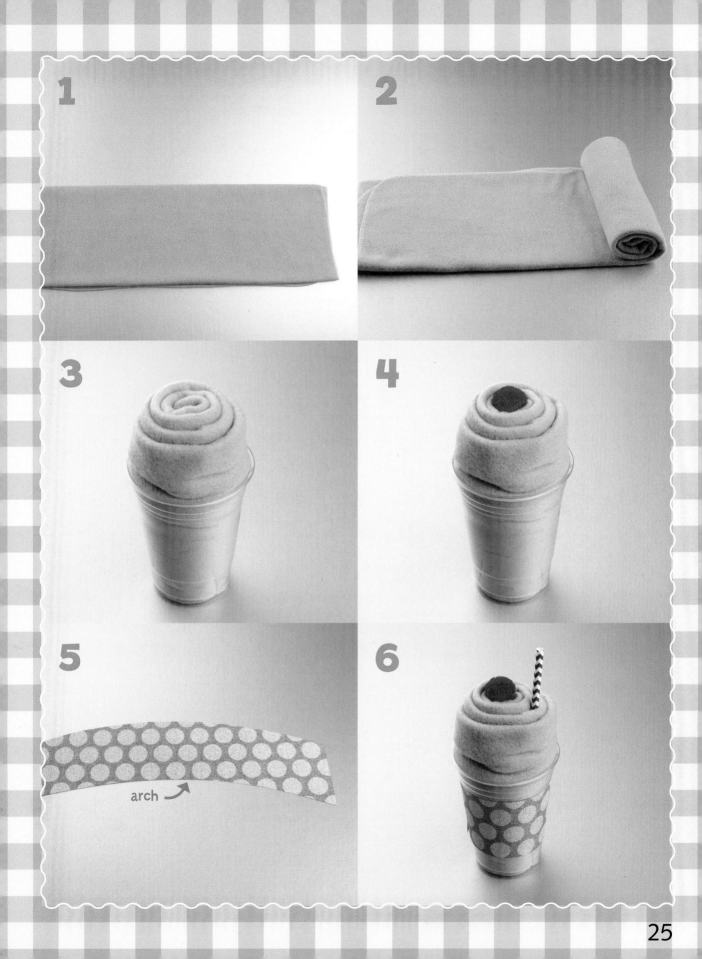

1

2

3

4

5

arch ↗

6

Felt Purse

This pretty little flower purse will be your favorite. The flower looks just like a rose from Miss Clarabelle's garden. Choose a matching button for the closure.

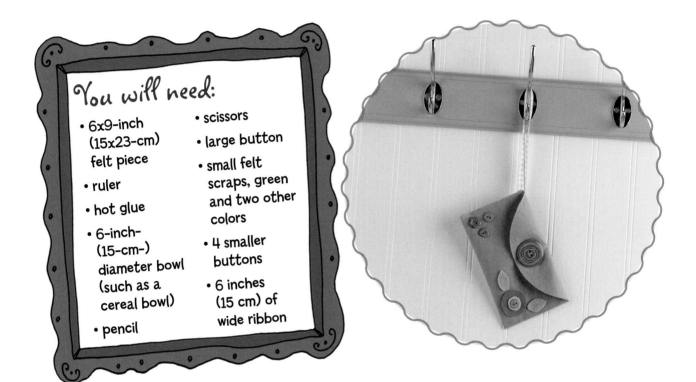

You will need:

- 6x9-inch (15x23-cm) felt piece
- ruler
- hot glue
- 6-inch- (15-cm-) diameter bowl (such as a cereal bowl)
- pencil
- scissors
- large button
- small felt scraps, green and two other colors
- 4 smaller buttons
- 6 inches (15 cm) of wide ribbon

1. Fold over 3 ½ inches (8.9 cm) of the long edge of the felt. Glue the sides together to form the purse's body.

2. To make the purse flap, place the bowl face down on the felt. The edge of the bowl should line up with the felt's top edge. Trace around the outside of the bowl to the left and right edges of the fold. Remove the bowl and cut on the trace line.

3. Glue a large button onto the purse under the center of the flap.

4. Fold the flap over the button. Cut a slit that's just big enough to go around the button.

5. Cut two small leaves from the green felt scraps. Cut a small circle from one color, and a smaller circle from the second color. Glue the leaves and two circles in one corner of the purse to make a flower.

6. Glue three small buttons onto the other corner of the purse and one onto the flower. Glue both ends of the ribbon to one top corner of the purse. This will be the strap.

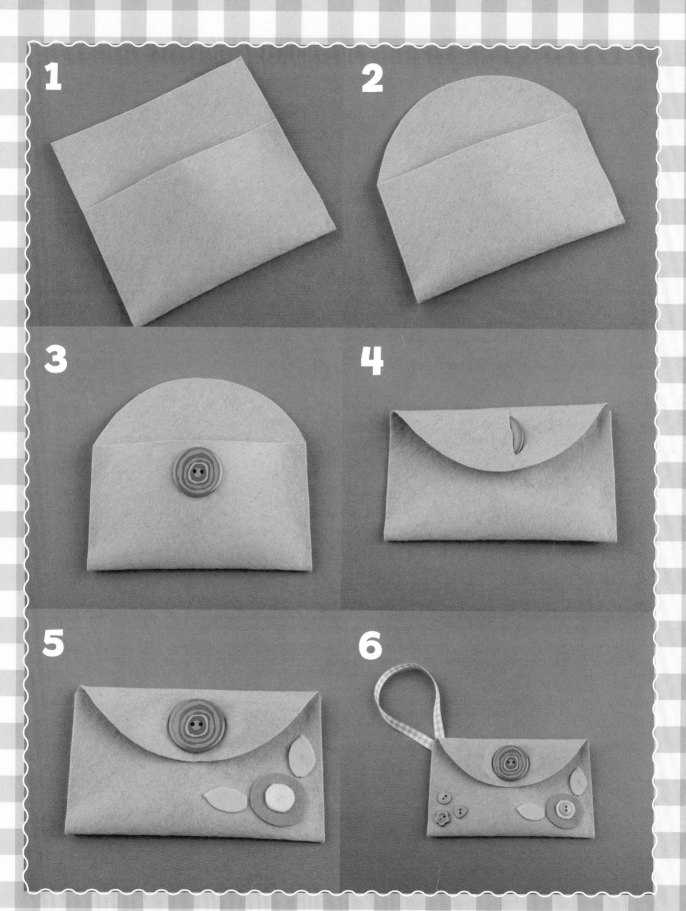

Princess Crown Piñata ☆

Piñatas are more fun than a picnic in June! This one is simple to make. You can get the candy and treats to put inside it at any dollar store.

You will need:

- 6 plastic bottle caps
- white glue
- glitter
- 2 or 3 sheets of 8 ½ x 11-inch (22x28-cm) white paper
- scissors
- masking tape
- cornmeal or oatmeal container
- chenille stem
- candies and treats
- crumpled newspaper
- 4x16-inch (10x41-cm) poster board
- ruler
- 3 sheets of 19x24-inch (48x61-cm) tissue paper
- 6 yards (5.5 m) of curling ribbon
- 2 yards (1.8 m) of string

1. Glue glitter to the tops of the plastic bottle caps. Let dry.

2. Cut the white paper to fit around the food container. Tape the seam.

3. Ask an adult to poke two holes in the container lid. Make a loop with a chenille stem. On the bottom side of the lid, twist the stem ends together to hold in place.

4. Fill the container with candies and treats. Add crumpled newspaper if it's not full. Tape around the lid.

5. Cut poster board to fit around the top of the container. Make six points like a crown. Tape it onto the container.

6. Cut about 10, 4-inch- (10-cm-) wide tissue paper strips. Fold them in half along the length, and cut fringe. Don't cut through the fold.

7. Glue a strip of tissue around the base of the container. Glue the next strip about 1 inch (2.5 cm) above the first strip, overlapping the first strip. Continue until you reach the top. For the points of the crown, cut smaller strips and fold over the edges. Glue to the backs of the points.

8. Glue a plastic bottle cap to each point.

9. Tape curled ribbon to the bottom of the container, and tie string to the chenille loop for hanging.

Cupcake Toppers

Cupcakes are so delicious! You can create these adorable cupcake toppers for your cupcakes. Be sure your guests know the cupcakes are for eating, but the toppers are decorations. Ugly Brother tried to eat the whole thing. Silly doggie!

You will need:

- 2, 3½-inch (8.9-cm) squares of scrapbook paper for each topper
- scissors
- 2-inch (5.1-cm) square colored paper for each topper
- white glue
- jewel crown sticker
- markers
- toothpicks
- 12 small rhinestones for each topper

Optional:
- rhinestone crown sticker

1. For each party guest, cut two flowers from the 3 ½-inch (8.9-cm) scrapbook paper squares. A cookie cutter makes a good pattern.

2. From the 2-inch (5.1-cm) colored paper squares, cut out two circles. Glue a circle to each of the flowers.

3. Place a crown sticker in the middle of one circle.

4. On the second circle, use markers to write the guest's name.

5. Glue the flowers back-to-back with the toothpick in between. Add small rhinestones around the circle on each side.

Optional: Add a rhinestone crown sticker above the guest's name.

Read More

Okui, Jessica. *Party Origami: Paper and Instructions for 14 Party-Themed Folds.* San Francisco: Chronicle Books, 2013.

Peschke, Marci. *Party Queen.* Kylie Jean. North Mankato, Minn.: Picture Window Books, 2013.

Rau, Dana Meachen. *Piece of Cake!: Decorating Awesome Cakes.* Dessert Designer. North Mankato, Minn.: Capstone Press, 2013.

Internet Sites

FactHound offers a safe, fun way to find Internet sites related to this book. All of the sites on FactHound have been researched by our staff.

Here's all you do:

Visit *www.facthound.com*

Type in this code: 9781479521913

Super-cool stuff! Check out projects, games and lots more at **www.capstonekids.com**

Look for all the books in the series:

Party Craft Queen   Rodeo Craft Queen

Pirate Craft Queen   Summer Camp Craft Queen